Steck Vaughn

Social Studies

MW00783802

Homes AND Families

PROGRAM CONSULTANTS

Sonya Abbye Taylor, Senior Associate
Professional Development Network, Inc.
(Education Consultant)
New Rochelle, N.Y.
and
Field Supervisor and Instructor
Manhattanville College
Purchase, N.Y.

Barbara C. Donahue, Principal
Burlington County Special Services School District
Westampton, N.J.

Harcourt Achieve

Rigby • Saxon • Steck-Vaughn

www.HarcourtAchieve.com
1.800.531.5015

ACKNOWLEDGMENTS

Photo Credits: P.5 ©Tom McCarthy/Unicorn Stock Photos; p.6 (top) ©Joan Menschenfreund, (bottom) ©Myrleen Ferguson Cate/PhotoEdit; p.8 ©Joan Menschenfreund; p.9 (top) ©Stephen McBrady/PhotoEdit, (bottom) ©Richard Hutchings; p.10 (all) ©Tony Freeman/PhotoEdit; p.11 (left) ©Tom McCarthy/Unicorn Stock Photos, (right) ©Tony Freeman/PhotoEdit; p.12 ©The Contemporary Forum, Chicago; p.15 (left) ©Joan Menschenfreund, (bottom) ©Eddie Rodriguez; p.16 (middle left) ©Erik Anderson/Stock Boston, (middle right) ©Ric Shoenbaum/Black Star, (bottom left) ©Eddie Rodriguez; p.17 (both) ©Joan Menschenfreund; p.18 (top) ©Joan Menschenfreund, (bottom) ©Eddie Rodriguez; p.19 (middle left) ©Michael Newman/PhotoEdit, (middle right) ©Peter Buckley, (bottom left) ©Jacques Jangoux/Peter Arnold; p.21 (left) ©David Young-Wolff/PhotoEdit, (right) ©Eric Berndt/Unicorn Stock Photos; p.23 ©Bob Daemmrich/The Image Works; p.25 (top) ©David Young-Wolff/PhotoEdit, (bottom) ©Michael Schwartz/The Image Works; p.26 (middle left) ©Michael Newman/PhotoEdit, (middle right) ©Richard Hutchings, (bottom right) ©Myron Wood/Photo Researchers; p.27 (middle left) ©Bob Daemmrich/The Image Works, (middle right) ©Robert Brent/PhotoEdit; p.28 (left) ©Eddie Rodriguez, (right) ©Bill Aron/PhotoEdit; p.30 (left) ©Peter Larsen/Photo Researchers, (middle right) ©Peter Buckley, (bottom right) ©Nevada Wier/CORBIS; p.32 (left) ©Mark Richards/PhotoEdit, (right) ©Patrick Dunn; p.33 ©J. Pickerell/The Image Works; p.34 (left) ©Bob Daemmrich/The Image Works, (middle right) ©David Young-Wolff/PhotoEdit, (bottom) ©Eric Bean/Getty Images; p.35 (left) ©Owen Franken/Stock Boston, (right) ©Myrleen Ferguson Cate/PhotoEdit; p.36 ©American Red Cross; p.42 ©Richard Hutchings; p.45 ©Bob Daemmrich/The Image Works; p.46 ©Joe Sohm/Visions of America; p.47 (left) ©Richard Hutchings, (right) ©Apple Computer, Inc.; p.50 (left) ©Michal Heron, (right) ©Clyde H. Smith/Peter Arnold, Inc.; p.53 (top) ©Patrick Dunn; p.54 ©John Neubauer/PhotoEdit; p.56 (left) ©Cary Wolinski/Stock Boston, (bottom) ©Tony Freeman/PhotoEdit; p.57 (top) ©Myrleen Ferguson Cate/PhotoEdit, (bottom) ©Lawrence Cherney/Getty Images; p.62 (top) ©Joan Menschenfreund, (bottom left) ©Richard Hutchings, (bottom right) ©James R. Holland/Stock Boston; p.63 Courtesy of The Historical Society of Pennsylvania Collection, Atwater Kent Museum of Philadelphia; p.64 ©Michal Heron; p.67 ©Joe Sohm/Visions of America; p.68 ©James Randlev/Getty Images; p.69 NASA; p.71 (top) ©Dwight Ellefsen/Superstock, (bottom) ©John Running/Stock Boston; p.72 ©Fred J. Maroon/Photo Researchers; p.73 (top) ©Oliver Ribbot/Stock Boston, (bottom) ©A. Ramey/Unicorn Stock Photos; p.74 ©Carl Frank/Photo Researchers; p.77 (left) ©David Edmonson/Superstock, (right) ©William Strode/Superstock; p.79 (middle right) ©Joan Menschenfreund, (bottom left) ©Jeff Greenberg/PhotoEdit, (bottom right) ©Michal Heron; p.80 (top) ©The National Archives, (middle left) ©Miro Vintoniv/Stock Boston, (middle right) ©Myrleen Ferguson Cate/PhotoEdit; p.81 ©L. Kilvoord/the Image Works; p.82 ©Sagamore Hill National Historic Site/National Park Service; p.85 ©James Randlev/Getty Images; p.86 ©David Ball/CORBIS; p.87 ©Michal Heron; p.88 (middle left) ©Francis G. Mayer/CORBIS, (middle right) ©National Museum of Natural History ©2004 Smithsonian Institution, (bottom) ©Smithsonian American Art Museum, Washington, DC/Art Resource, NY; p.89 ©Smithsonian American Art Museum, Washington, DC/Art Resource, NY; p.90 (top) ©National Museum of Natural History ©2004 Smithsonian Institution, (bottom) ©Smithsonian American Art Museum, Washington, DC/Art Resource, NY; p.92 ©John Hancock Mutual Life Insurance Company; p.93 ©Tom McCarthy/PhotoEdit; p.97 (bottom right) ©Lawrence Migdale/Stock Boston, (left) ©Roy Morsch/CORBIS; p.98 ©Tony Freeman/PhotoEdit; p.99 ©Eddie Rodriguez; p.100 ©Joan Menschenfreund; p.102 (top) ©Carl Frank/Photo Researchers, (bottom left) ©Gideon Mendel/CORBIS; p.103 ©Joan Menschenfreund; p.105 ©David Ball/CORBIS; p.109 (top) ©Lawrence Migdale/Stock Boston, (middle) NASA, (bottom) ©Joan Menschenfreund; p.110 ©Tony Freeman/PhotoEdit; p.111 ©The National Archives; p.112 (top) ©David Edmonson/Superstock (bottom) ©Smithsonian American Art Museum, Washington, DC/Art Resource, NY.

Additional photography by Getty Images Royalty Free, Royalty-Free/CORBIS, and Superstock Royalty Free.

ISBN: 0-7398-9218-5

3 4 5 6 7 8 9 030 10 09 08 07 06

Contents

UNIT 1

Families

People live in families.
Families are alike and different.

- How are they alike?
- How are they different?

UNIT PROJECT

Work with a team.
Cut out pictures of families from magazines.
Find pictures of small families and large families.
Bring pictures of your family.
Tell your classmates about your family.

What Is a Family?

How big is your **family?**
Some families are large.
Some families are small.
Look at the pictures.

Circle the large family.

Put a blue ✔ next to the small family.

Is your family large?
Is your family small?

 Draw a picture of your family.

Draw your picture here.

My Family

We need families.
Families help us.
Families give us love.
Look at the picture.

Circle the person who is helping.

Who is being helped?

Draw a line under the person.

Who helps you?

Write your answer here.

_____

- - - - - - - - - - - - -

_____

_____

- - - - - - - - - - - - -

_____

8

Families help in many ways.
They give us homes.
They give us clothes.
They give us food.

Look at each picture.

Who is buying food?

Put a red ✔ next to the picture.

Who is making clothes?

Put a green ✔ next to the picture.

Families change.
Families get bigger.
Look at the pictures.
How has the family changed?

Which picture is the first taken of this family?

Write 1 in the box.

Which picture comes next?

Write 2 in the box.

Which picture shows the family as it is now?

Write 3 in the box.

10

Families change in other ways, too.
Families move to new homes.
Moms and dads get new jobs.
Children go to new schools.

Look at each picture.

Do the pictures show how a family changes?

Put a ✔ over each picture that shows change.

UNIT PROJECT Tip

Ask your family for pictures.
Find pictures of your family having fun together.
Find pictures that show how your family has changed.
Bring the pictures to class.

Gwendolyn Brooks was a poet.
She grew up in Chicago.
Gwendolyn never forgot what it was like growing up.
She wrote poems about it.
Some of her poems are about children and families.
Some poems are about things that families do.

What would you write about being in a family?

Write your answer here.

Keeping in Touch

Families do not always live together. Families still want to know about each other.

■ **Look at the pictures.**

How does your family keep in touch?

Put a ✔ next to ways your family uses.

13

Which picture shows a family?

Circle the family picture.

Look at the picture of the family below.

Draw a line over the two oldest people.

Put an X over the youngest person.

THINKING AND WRITING

Tell one way families change.
Write your answer here.

_____

_ _ _ _ _ _ _ _ _ _ _ _ _ _ _ _ _ _ _

_____

Families Work and Play Together

Families work together.
They work at home.
Everyone can help.

Who is helping?

Write your answer here.

_____

— — — — — — — — — — — — — — —

_____

The boy is helping.
He can make his bed.

How do you help?

Write your answer here.

_____

— — — — — — — — — — — — — — —

_____

15

Families play together.
They play at home and away.
They have fun.
Look at the pictures.

Put a ✔ on the family at home.

Draw a line under the families having fun away from home.

Families have **rules.**
Rules tell us what to do and what
not to do.
Families have clean-up rules.
They have safety rules.

Look at the pictures.

**What kind of rule does each picture
show?**

Write your answer under each picture.

_____

- - - - - - - - - - - - - - - -

_____

_____

- - - - - - - - - - - - - - - -

_____

UNIT
PROJECT
Tip
Talk to your family about rules at home.
What rules do you have?
Think about why these rules are important.

17

Families have bedtime rules.
One rule is the hour we go to bed.
Another rule is to wash before bed.
We need rest to be healthy.

Read these rules.

Put a ✔ next to some bedtime rules.

Go to bed at a good hour. _____

Put your toys away. _____

Eat a healthy snack. _____

Brush your teeth. _____

Families Together

Families live in many places.
They live all around the world.
They work together.
They play together.
They have fun on special days.
Look at the pictures.

Circle a family working.

Draw a line under a family having fun on a special day.

19

Look at the pictures.

Put a ✔ under a family having fun.

Draw a line under a picture that shows a safety rule.

Why do we need rules?
Write your answer here.

_____

- -

_____

- -

_____

Learning About Alike and Different

Think about families.
Think about your own family.
Think about other families you know.
How are families alike?
How are families different?

Put a ✔ by one way families are alike.

Families help us. _____

Families do not work at home. _____

Put a ✔ by one way families are different.

Families buy food. _____

Families are large or small. _____

Now it's time to finish your project.
Talk with your team.
Answer these questions.

- **How are families alike?**

- **How are families different?**

- **How do families change?**

Work with your team. Try one of these ideas.

➤ Make a book called "Families Are Alike and Different." Each member of your team will make a page for the book. Add the pictures you brought from home to your page. Talk about what is alike and different about the families of your team members.

➤ Work with your team to make a mural. Draw pictures of your families having fun together at a picnic or in a park. Write the names of your family members on the mural.

UNIT 2

Families Have Needs and Wants

We must have food to live.

- What are some other things we must have?

- What are some things people want?

- Who works to give us these things?

UNIT PROJECT

Work with a team.
Think about needs and wants.
Look for pictures that show needs and wants families have.

What Do Families Need and Want?

Families need and want many things.
A **need** is something you must have
to live.
A **want** is something you would like
to have.

Look at the pictures.

Draw a circle around needs.

Put a ✔ on wants.

All families need food.
Families get food from different places.
We grow food.
We buy food.
We cook food.

 Draw a line from each sentence to the picture it tells about.

We buy food.

We grow food.

Families need homes.
Some homes are tall.
Some homes are small.
Some homes can be moved.
All homes keep us warm and dry.
Look at the pictures.

Circle a tall home.

Draw a line under a home that can be moved.

Families need clothing.
We buy clothes.
We make clothes.
We share clothes that are too small
for us.
Look at the pictures.

Circle someone who is buying clothes.

Families have wants.
They want to do things to have fun.
They want to have things they like.
Food and clothing are needs.
They can be wants, too.
Look at the pictures.

Circle the picture of something someone wants.

Draw a line under the picture of things that can be wants and needs.

UNIT PROJECT Tip

Work with your team.
Draw three needs.
Draw three wants.
Keep the paper for your team's book.

Families need food, clothing, and a
place to live.
Families want other things, too.
Look at the picture.
What does it show?

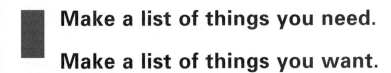 **Make a list of things you need.**

Make a list of things you want.

I need	I want

All Families Need Food

Families live all over the world.
Some families live near us.
Some families live far, far away.
All families, near and far, need food.
Look at the pictures.

Put an X on the family eating with their hands.

Draw a line over the family eating with chopsticks.

Circle the people who are shopping for food.

CHAPTER ✓ CHECKUP

Write an N on things we need.

 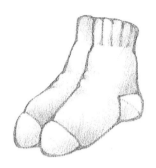  

Circle the places where people live.

 Is a new bike a need or a want?
Write your answer here.

_____

_ _ _ _ _ _ _ _ _ _ _ _ _ _ _ _ _ _ _ _

_____

31

Families at Work

Families work.
Families work to earn money.
They use money to buy things they need and want.
Some people work at home.
Look at the two pictures.

Put a ✔ on the picture of the farmer.

Draw a line under the picture of the babysitter.

People work away from home.
Some work in a store.
Some work in a factory.
Look at the picture.
Is this a store or a factory?

 Circle the answer.

   store   **factory**

What do people do in a factory?

 Circle the answer.

They make things.   **They sell things.**

 Bring or draw a picture for your team's book.
Show how someone you know works.

People work to help us.
Some work to keep us safe.
Some work to help us learn.
Look at the pictures.

Who helps us learn in school?

Circle two pictures.

Who works to keep us safe?

Draw a line under one picture.

Children can earn money, too.
They can do jobs for family and
neighbors.
All people can earn money.
Then they can buy things they need and
want.
Look at the pictures.
What work are the children doing?
What kinds of work can children do?

What work would you like to do?

Write your answer here.

_____

- -

_____

Clara Barton

Clara Barton lived long ago.
She was a nurse.
She worked to help sick people.
She started the American Red Cross.
The Red Cross helps people around the world.
It helps people hurt by big storms and floods.
Today men and women are nurses.
Do you know a nurse?

 Draw a picture of a nurse who has helped you.

Draw your picture here.

Read each question.

Find a picture it matches.

Write the number in the box above the correct picture.

1. Who helps at home?

2. Who helps us learn to do things?

Name one worker who keeps us healthy.
Name one worker who helps us learn something.
Write your answers on the lines.

_____

_____

_____

_____

37

Families Make Choices

Families choose the things they need.
They choose a home.
Look at the picture.

Is this a good place for a family?

Say why.

Write your answer here.

_____

- - - - - - - - - - - - - - - -

_____

- - - - - - - - - - - - - - - -

_____

- - - - - - - - - - - - - - - -

_____

Some families choose to live in tall buildings.
The buildings have room for many families.
Other families choose to live in houses.

Look at the picture.

Who lives here?

Circle the answer.

one family   **many families**

Families need and want many things.
Some families need cars.
How do they choose a car?

■ **Circle the car that this family should choose.**

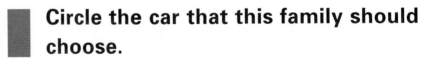
Work with your team.
Find or draw more pictures for your book.
Show some homes people choose.

Families want many things.
They cannot have everything they want.

Why not?

Write your answer here.

_____

- -

_____

_____

- -

_____

A Way to Choose

Sometimes people want different things.
Look at the picture.
Some children want to sing one song.
Others want to sing a different song.
What will they do?
They will vote.
Voting is fair.
It lets everyone help choose.

Did you ever vote?

Write about it here.

_____

_____

_____

A family must choose the
things it needs.
Look at the pictures.
A family needs a place to live.
What does the family choose?
Circle the answer.

A family needs food.
What do they choose?
Put an X on the food they need.

 THINKING AND WRITING Why must a family choose what to buy?
Write your answer here.

_____

- - - - - - - - - - - - - - - - - - -

_____

- - - - - - - - - - - - - - - - - - -

_____

Making a List

Find two pictures that show needs.
Write them on the NEEDS list.
Find two pictures that show wants.
Write them on the WANTS list.
Draw one more want and one more need
in the two empty boxes.
Add their names to your lists.

NEEDS	WANTS
1. _____	1. _____
2. _____	2. _____
3. _____	3. _____

PRESENT YOUR PROJECT

Now it's time to present your project.
Talk with your team.
Answer these questions.

- **What are needs?**

- **What are wants?**

- **How do people get money for needs and wants?**

- **How do people choose what to buy?**

Work with your team. Try one of these ideas.

➤ Put your pictures together in a book. Ask your teacher to help you tie the pages together. Make a cover. Put your names on it. Show your book to other teams.

➤ Put your pictures together. Place them on big pieces of colored paper. Tell about your pictures. Put them on a bulletin board.

UNIT 3

Where We Live, Work, and Play

People live in all kinds of places.
Think about the place where you live.

- Are there homes for many people?
- Are there places to work and play?

UNIT PROJECT

Work with a team.
Make a scrapbook about
your neighborhood.
Find or write stories and
pictures.

Your School

We go to school.
It is a place to work and play.
We learn many things in school.

**Read the sentences below.
Circle the sentences that tell what you
do in school.**

I play with friends.

I learn to read and write.

I sleep.

I learn to share.

I work with my teacher.

Here is a picture of a classroom.
This is where we work in school.

Find the right side of the classroom.

What is on top of the table?

Circle the answer.

rabbit   **paints**   **ball**

Find the left side of the classroom.

What is on the wall?

rabbit   **books**   **window**

This is a picture of the same classroom.

What is near the teacher's desk?

Write your answer here.

_____

- - - - - - - - - - - - - - - - - - - -

_____

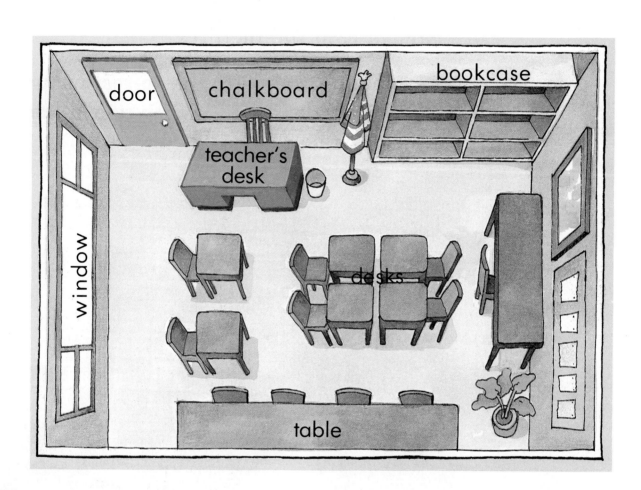

Find the flag.

What do you see next to the flag?

Write your answer here.

_____

- - - - - - - - - - - - - - - - - - - -

_____

We have rules in school.
Rules tell us what to do.
Rules tell us what not to do.
Read the rules.

1. We work quietly.

2. We give other people a turn.

Now look at the pictures.

**Match each rule to the correct picture.
Write the number of each rule in the
correct box.**

 Find or draw pictures of your school.
Keep them for your scrapbook.

We need rules.

Rules help us live together.

Rules help keep us safe.

Rules make things fair.

Look at the picture.

What rule is the boy breaking?

_____

- - - - - - - - - - - - - - - - - - - -

_____

- - - - - - - - - - - - - - - - - - - -

_____

Which rule helps you the most? Why?

_____

- - - - - - - - - - - - - - - - - - - -

_____

- - - - - - - - - - - - - - - - - - - -

_____

Most schools have a playground.
This is where you play at school.
Look at the picture of this playground.
There are trees and slides.

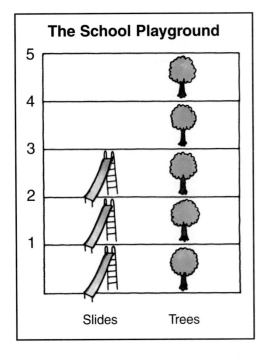

Look at the **picture graph.**
The picture graph shows
how many.

**How many trees are
on the picture graph?
Write your answer here.**

————
– – – – –
————

**How many slides
do you see?
Write your answer here.**

————
– – – – –
————

Who helps us at school?
The librarian helps us find books.
The teacher helps us learn to read them.
Look at the pictures.

 Who is helping?

Write the answer next to each picture.

Children Go to School

Children go to school all over the world.
In Mexico people speak Spanish.
The Spanish word for school is *escuela*.
Mexican children go to an *escuela* to learn.

Look at the picture.
Does the school in Mexico look like your school?

Draw a picture of your school here.

Look at the picture.

1. Who helps children learn?
Draw a line under the person.

2. Look at the right side of the picture.
Circle the class pet.

3. What is behind the teacher's desk?
Put an X on it.

Why does this class need rules?
Write your answer here.

_____

- -

_____

Families Live in Neighborhoods

What is a **neighborhood?**
It is where families live.
It is where families work and play.
Look at the pictures.

Put a ✔ next to a neighborhood.

Put an X next to a place to work.

Draw a line over a place to play.

There are many kinds of neighborhoods.
Some neighborhoods are in the city.
Some are in the country.
Look at the two pictures.

 How are these neighborhoods alike?

_____

- -

_____

_____

- -

_____

Look at the picture on these two pages.
It is a picture of a neighborhood.
There are places to live, work, and play.
What places can you find?

 **Find a place to play.
Circle it.**

**Find a place to buy food.
Draw a line under it.**

**Find a place where many people
can live.
Put a ✔ next to it.**

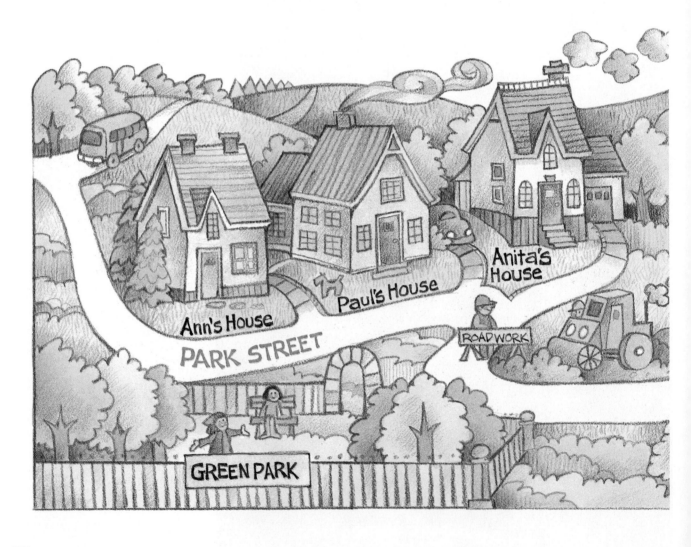

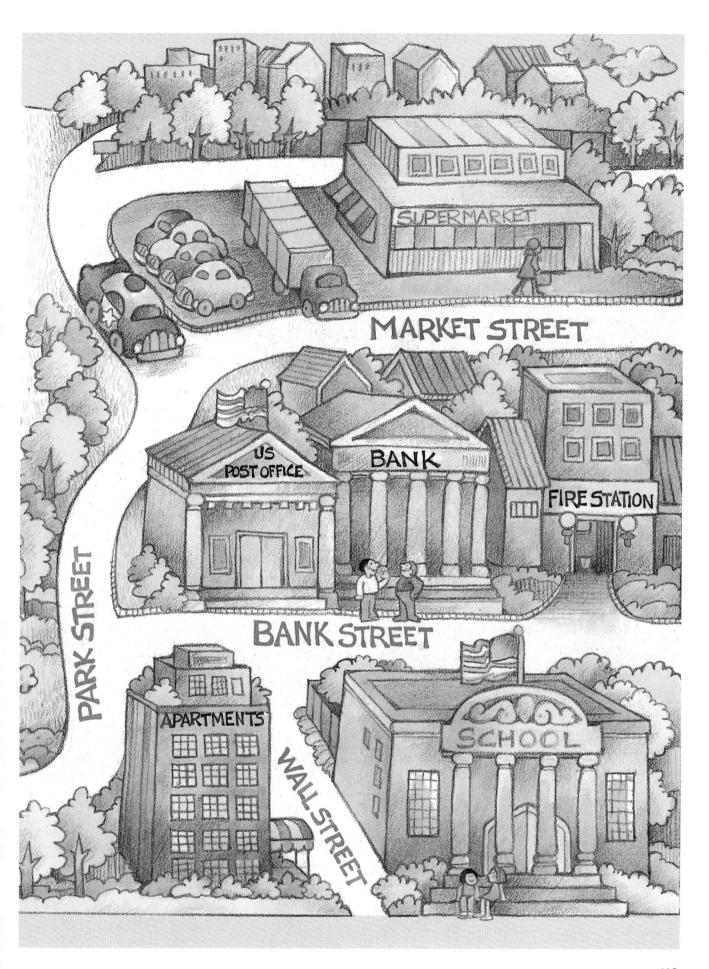

This is a **map** of the same neighborhood. A map is a special drawing of a place. The **map key** tells what the pictures on the map mean.

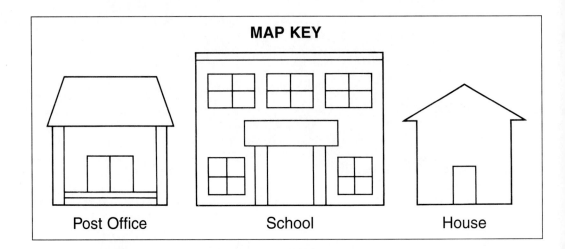

MAP KEY

Post Office   School   House

 Look at the map key above.

Find the picture for house.
Put a ✔ under it.

Find the picture for school.
Draw a line under it.

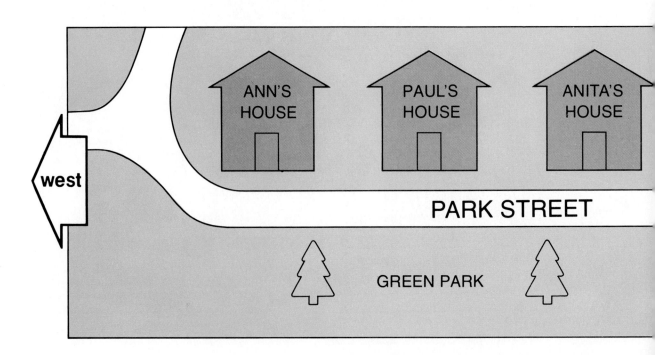

Find the arrows on the map.
These arrows show **directions.**
Directions show the way to go.
North, south, east, and west are
directions.

What is east of Wall Street?
Draw a line under it.

What place is south of Park Street?
Circle it.

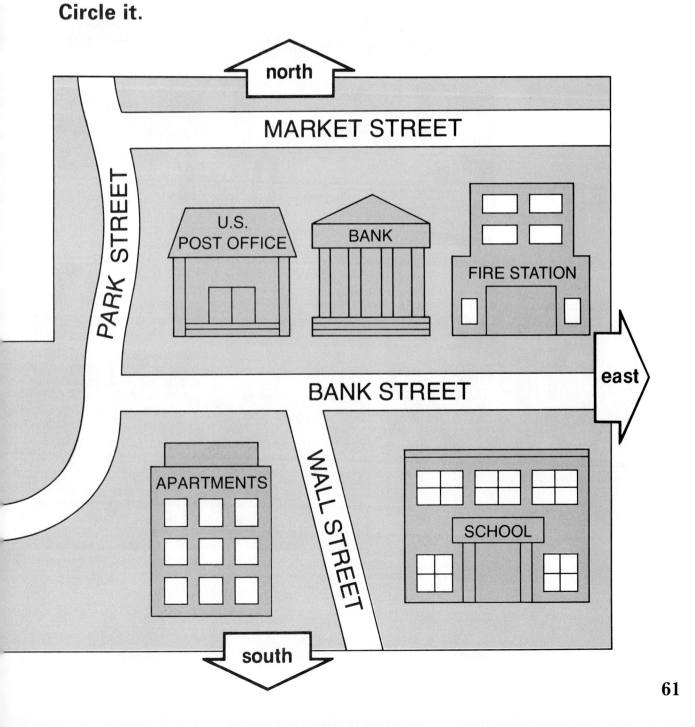

61

These pictures show how neighborhoods change.

Which family is moving?

Put a red ✔ next to the picture.

Who is planting a garden?

Draw a line under the picture.

Find out about places people work in your neighborhood.
Write about what people do there.

Benjamin Franklin lived long, long ago.
He lived in the city of Philadelphia.
There was no hospital for sick people.
There was no library to get books.
Mr. Franklin helped build a hospital and library.
He helped many, many families.

 Do you use the library?

Draw a map of your library here.

Draw a map key, too.

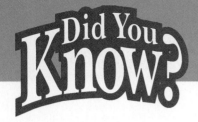

Long ago, families built their own homes.
They built places to work, too.
Today, you can visit some of these places.
You can see how families lived long ago.
You can learn how families and places have changed.
You can learn how families and places have stayed the same.

Look at the picture.

What would you ask someone who lived here long ago?

Write your question here.

_____

_____

_____

Read the words in the box.
Write each word next to the correct picture.

| map key   neighborhood   map |

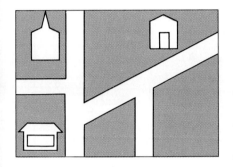

_____

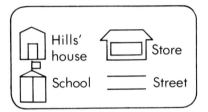

_____

_____

THINKING AND WRITING In what ways can a neighborhood change?
Write your answer here.

_____

Using a Map Key

Remember that a map is a special drawing of a place.

Look at the map and map key.

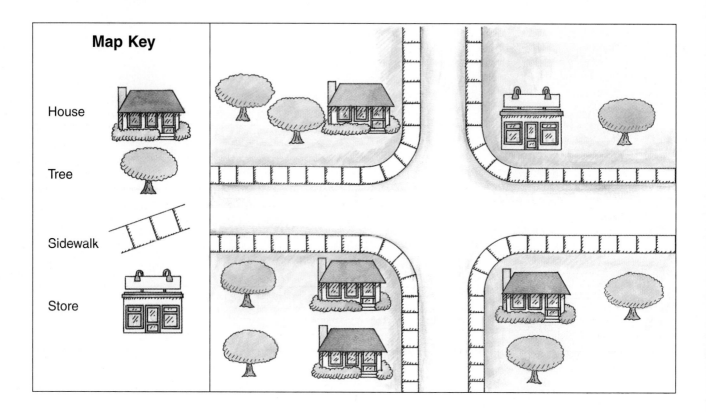

1. Find a sidewalk on the map.
   Color it red.

2. Find the store on the map.
   Put a blue X on the store.

3. How many houses are in the neighborhood?
   Write your answer here.

_____

- - - - - - - - - - - - - - -

_____

Now it is time to finish your project.
Talk with your team.
Answer these questions.

- **What kinds of places are in your neighborhood?**

- **What does your school look like?**

- **What work do people do in your neighborhood?**

Work with your team.
Try one of these ideas.

➤ Put your pictures together. Make a scrapbook of your neighborhood. Add stories that tell about the places.

➤ Tell classmates about your neighborhood. Show the pictures of your neighborhood.

➤ Each student tell a story about one picture.

UNIT 4

Our Country's Land and Water

People live in many kinds of places.
Some places are hot and sunny.
Some places are near water.

- What kinds of places do you know about?

- What do people do there?

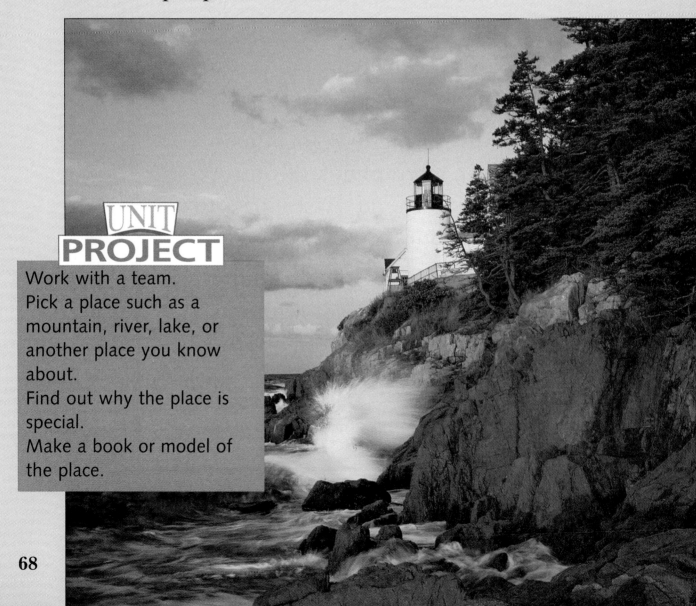

UNIT PROJECT

Work with a team.
Pick a place such as a mountain, river, lake, or another place you know about.
Find out why the place is special.
Make a book or model of the place.

CHAPTER 8

Families Live in Different Places

This is a picture of **Earth.**
We live on Earth.
The white parts are clouds.
The blue parts are water.
The brown parts are land.

Earth is not flat.
It is round like a ball.

 Can you see both sides of Earth at one time?
Circle the answer.

yes   no

These are pictures of a **globe.**
A globe is round like Earth.
But a globe is much, much smaller.
You can hold a globe in your hands.
You can see water and land on a globe.

 What color is the water?

Circle the answer.

blue   **green**

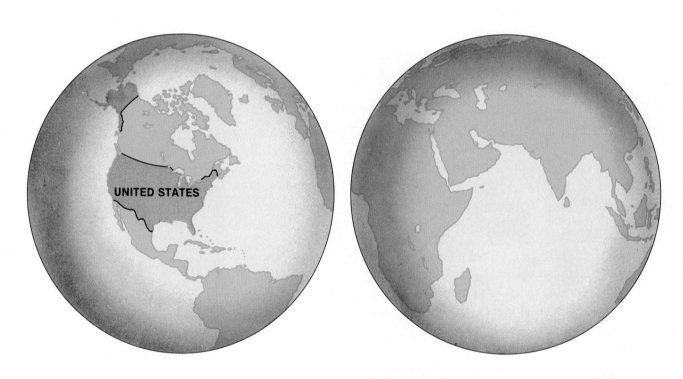

 Find the United States on the globe.

Circle the United States.

 Look at pictures in books of the place your
team chose.
Draw pictures of what the place looks like.
What plants, animals, and people live there?

Earth is very big.
Families live in many places.
Some families live on farms.
These farms are on flat land.
Other families live near **mountains.**
A mountain is very high land.
Look at the pictures.

Put a red ✔ next to the farm.

Put a green ✔ next to the mountains.

Some families live near water.
They may live near **rivers.**
A river is water that flows across the land.
What is the place like where you live?
Is the land flat or is it high?
Is there water where you live?

 Draw a picture of where you live.

Draw your picture here.

People work in many places.
Some people work on the water.
Some people work high in the air.
Where would you like to work?
Look at the pictures.

 Who is working on the water?

Put a red ✔ next to the picture.

Who is working high in the air?

Put a blue ✔ next to the picture.

People work all over the world.
Look at the picture of the farmer.
He lives in Mexico.
He is planting corn.

Circle what the man is planting.

 Read the sentences below.
Circle the sentence that tells about the picture.

The farm is on flat land.

The farm is on a mountain.

The farm is on a beach.

Some people leave Earth for a short time.
They go into space in special ships.
Space is all around Earth.
People can work in space.
They learn about Earth and other things.
Then they come back to Earth.

 What would you like to know about space?

Write your question here.

_____

- -

_____

Read each question.
Circle the correct answer.

1. What is the shape of Earth?

round   flat   square

2. What color is water on a globe?

brown   blue   white

3. Which can you hold in
your hand?

globe   Earth   mountain

4. What is the place like where
you live?

in the mountains   on flat land   near water

THINKING AND WRITING Why are most farms on flat land and not mountains?

_____

_____

_____

_____

_____

Taking Care of Our Resources

The United States has many **resources.**
Resources are things found on Earth.
They are things like land, trees, and
water.
Even air is a resource.
Look at the pictures.

Tell what resource is in each picture.

Write your answer below each picture.

Resources are in all parts of the United
States.
Look at the map of the United States.

 **In what part of the United States do
you live?**

Put an X near where you live.

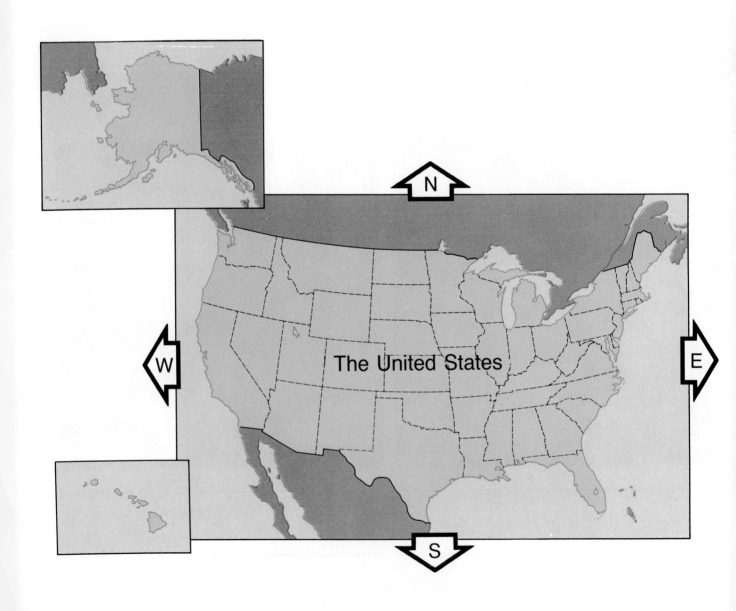

The United States

People cannot make resources.
So we must take care of them.
Plants, animals, and clean air are
resources all people use.
The pictures show some resources.
Show where we find them.
Use the map on page 78.

 Picture 1 shows large trees.

These trees grow in the West.

Put a red ✔ in the West on the map.

Picture 2 shows clean water in a river.

This river is in the South.

Put a blue ✔ in the South on the map.

Picture 3 shows good land for farming.

This land is in the North.

Put a green ✔ in the North on the map.

We need clean water, land, and air.
Pollution makes water, land, and air dirty.
Pollution hurts living things.
Pollution hurts our resources.

 Put a red ✔ next to clean resources.

Put a blue ✔ next to a picture of pollution.

How can we stop pollution?
We can stop making more pollution.
We can pick up cans.
We can throw things we do not
want into a basket.
We can ask others to help.
People around the world can help.

 Make a sign.
Tell people to help stop pollution.

Draw your sign here.

What resources does your place have?
Talk with your team about why it is important
to keep land, water, and air clean.
How do clean water and land look different
from polluted water and land?

Theodore Roosevelt was the 26th President of the United States a long time ago.

He cared about our resources.

He made places safe for birds and other animals to live.

Mr. Roosevelt also started big parks around the United States.

Many people visit these parks every year.

 What can you do to keep our resources safe?

Write your answers here.

_____

- - - - - - - - - - - - - - - - - -

_____

_____

- - - - - - - - - - - - - - - - - -

_____

_____

- - - - - - - - - - - - - - - - - -

_____

_____

- - - - - - - - - - - - - - - - - -

_____

CHAPTER ✓ CHECKUP

Look at the pictures.
Write the name of each resource below.
Use two words from the box.

water	bird	land

_____

- - - - - - - - - - - - - - - - - -

_____

_____

- - - - - - - - - - - - - - - - - -

_____

Why should people all over the world stop pollution?
Write your answer here.

_____

- -

_____

_____

- -

_____

Unit 4 Skill Builder

Using a United States Map

Look at the map of the United States.

1. Circle the arrow that points North.

2. Color the land brown.

3. Color one state in the South green.

4. Color all the water blue.

5. Draw a tree in the West.

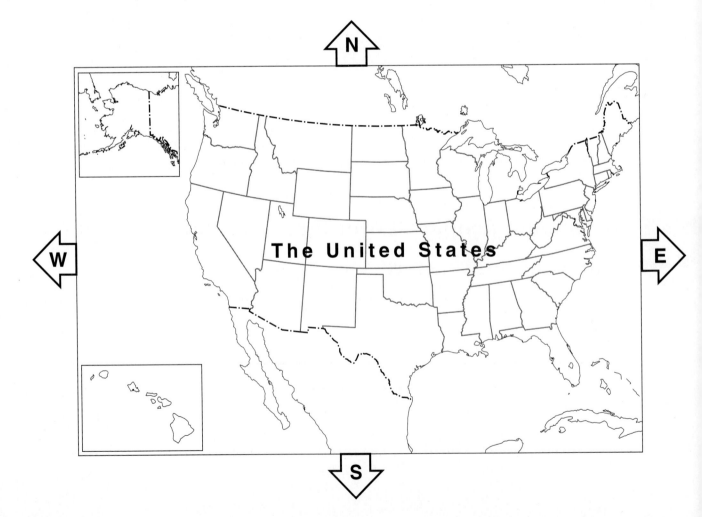

Now it is time to finish your project.
Talk with your team.
Answer these questions.

- **What plants, animals, and people live in the place your team chose?**

- **What resources does your place have?**

- **Why is it important to keep land, water, and air clean?**

Work with your team.
Try one of these ideas.

➤ Make a model of your place on a flat piece of cardboard. Use clay, sticks, colored paper, and other things. Show your model to another team. Tell them about the resources in your place.

➤ Make a picture book about your team's place. Draw pictures of the resources. Draw animals and people that live there. Write a sentence on each page telling about the picture. Show your book to another team. Take turns reading the sentences out loud.

Families Long Ago and Today

The first Americans were American Indians.
They came to America long, long ago.

- How did American Indian families find homes, food, and clothing?

- How did American Indians help other families who came to America?

- How do families share holidays?

UNIT PROJECT

Work with a team.
Learn about a holiday that families share.
Find or draw pictures about the holiday.
Find out what people do on the holiday.

First American Families

Many American Indians live in America.
They have lived here a long, long time.
They built homes and made clothes.
They hunted and fished for food.
They showed their children many things.

Look at the picture.
The girl is learning to make cloth.

Who is teaching the girl?

Write your answer here.

_____

_ _ _ _ _ _ _ _ _ _ _ _ _ _ _ _ _ _ _

_____

How did American Indians live long ago?
There were no stores then.
They grew food.
They hunted and fished.
Some made clothing from the skins of animals.

Find the picture of American Indians growing food.

Put a ✔ on the picture.

Find the American Indians fishing.

Put an X on the picture.

Look at the picture of an American
Indian village.
These American Indians lived in homes
called **tepees.**

 **Put an X on the tepees that are far
away.**

Put a ✔ on the tepee that is far left.

 Long ago, American Indians shared one holiday
with some new Americans.
You will find out about this holiday.
Do you know what it is?

American Indians lived in all parts of the United States.
They had different kinds of homes.
They made their homes from things they found where they lived.
Some families made homes of wood.
Some families made homes of grass.
Other families made homes of animal skins.

 Pretend it is long ago.

What is your home made of?

Draw a picture of what your home might look like.

CHAPTER CHECKUP

Read the sentences below.
Circle the sentences that are true.

The first Americans were American Indians.

Long, long ago, American Indians bought their food in stores.

American Indians made their clothes.

American Indians hunted animals for food.

Some American Indians farmed.

All American Indians lived in tepees.

How is an American Indian family of long ago like your family?
Write your answer here.

_____

- -

_____

- -

_____

Families and the First Thanksgiving

Long ago, the Pilgrims came to America.
They grew food.
They hunted and fished.
American Indians helped the Pilgrims.
The Pilgrims and American Indians
shared the first Thanksgiving.

Look at the picture.

What is one thing that is happening?

Write your answer here.

_____

_ _

_____

_____

_ _

_____

Today, families still share Thanksgiving.
Thanksgiving is in November.
Some families have big, big dinners.
They eat special foods.
They have friends visit.

What does your family do on Thanksgiving?

Write about your Thanksgiving here.

_____

_ _ _ _ _ _ _ _ _ _ _ _ _ _ _ _ _ _ _

_____

_____

_ _ _ _ _ _ _ _ _ _ _ _ _ _ _ _ _ _ _

_____

UNIT PROJECT Tip

What holiday did American Indian families share?
Draw a picture of Thanksgiving.

Look at the **chart** below.
A chart has facts in order.
The facts are listed in a table.
This chart tells about the first Thanksgiving.
It also tells about Thanksgiving today.

	First Thanksgiving	Thanksgiving Today
People	Pilgrims and American Indians	friends and family
Food	hunted for turkey	buy turkey in store
Time	three days	one day

Read the chart.

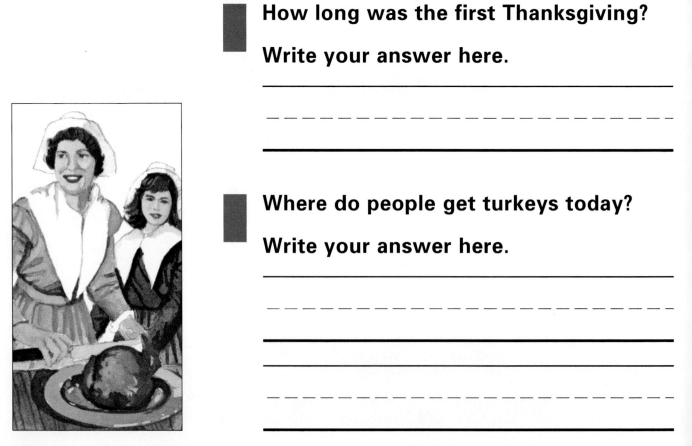

How long was the first Thanksgiving?

Write your answer here.

_____

— — — — — — — — — — — — — — — —

_____

Where do people get turkeys today?

Write your answer here.

_____

— — — — — — — — — — — — — — — —

_____

— — — — — — — — — — — — — — — —

_____

Squanto was an American Indian.
He lived long ago.
He helped the Pilgrims.
The Pilgrims were new to America.
They did not know how to live here.
Squanto showed the Pilgrims how to
grow corn.
He showed them how to catch fish.
He helped them get syrup from trees.

**What would have happened to the
Pilgrims without Squanto's help?**

Write your answer here.

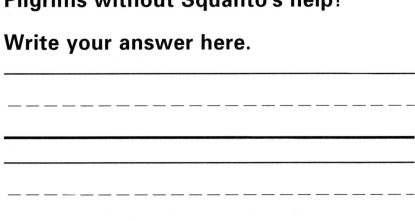

**Draw a picture here of Squanto helping
the Pilgrims.**

Read the sentences. Circle the sentences that are true.

Thanksgiving is in April.

Squanto helped the Pilgrims.

Today, Thanksgiving lasts three days.

The Pilgrims hunted their turkeys.

Pilgrims and American Indians shared the first Thanksgiving.

THINKING AND WRITING Why did the Pilgrims share Thanksgiving with the American Indians?
Write your answer here.

_____

- -

_____

- -

_____

- -

_____

- -

Ways We Celebrate and Remember

Families get together on special days
called **holidays.**
Families **celebrate** on these days.
Celebrate means to remember a special
day.
Some families celebrate Christmas.
They trim a tree.
Some families celebrate Hanukkah.
They light candles.
Some families celebrate Kwanzaa.
They light candles, too.

What is one holiday that your family celebrates? Write the name here.

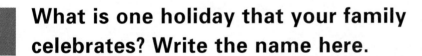

Look at the parade!
It is the Fourth of July.
It is the birthday of our country.
Do you see the flags in the picture?
They are flags of the United States.

How does your family celebrate the Fourth of July?

The flag stands for our country.
The flag makes us think of the United
States.

Look at the flag.
There are 50 stars on the flag.

How many red stripes are on the flag?

Write your answer here.

_____

- -

_____

**How many white stripes are on
the flag?**

Write your answer here.

_____

- -

_____

This is the Liberty Bell.
It makes us think of our country, too.
The Liberty Bell is over 200 years old.
It is in the city of Philadelphia.
Philadelphia is in the state of
Pennsylvania.

Look around your school.

What do you see that makes you think of the United States?

Write your answer here.

_____

– – – – – – – – – – – – – – – – – – – –

_____

UNIT PROJECT Tip

What are some things people do to celebrate
the Fourth of July?
Find or draw pictures of this holiday.
How do you celebrate this holiday?

Did You Know?

Caring for the Flag

We must take care of our flag.
There is a special way.
Match each sentence to the correct picture.

1. We raise the flag.

2. We salute the flag.

3. We fold the flag.

☐

☐

☐

Families Celebrate

Families live all over the world.
Families love their own countries.
They celebrate their own holidays.

What are some holidays your family celebrates?

Make a list here.

_____

- - - - - - - - - - - - - - - - - -

_____

- - - - - - - - - - - - - - - - - -

_____

- - - - - - - - - - - - - - - - - -

_____

Circle the colors of our flag.

      red   green   white   blue

What is the birthday of the United States?
Circle the correct answer.

      Fourth of July   Christmas   Hanukkah

Do families all over the world celebrate holidays?
Circle the correct answer.

      yes   no

What do you think of when you see the flag?
Write your answer here.

_____

- -

_____

THINKING AND WRITING What are two ways families celebrate holidays?
Write your answer here.

_____

- -

_____

- -

_____

Unit 5 Skill Builder
Reading a Chart

A chart lists facts in a table.
Look at the chart.

Some United States Holidays		
Holiday	What is celebrated	Month it is celebrated
Presidents' Day	Birthdays of two of our Presidents	February
Flag Day	United States flag	June
Earth Day	Land, water, and air on Earth	April

Answer each question.
Write your answers on the lines.

1. When is Earth Day celebrated?

_____

2. What holiday is celebrated in February?

_____

3. What holiday could you add to the chart?

_____

Now it is time to finish your project.
Talk with your classmates.
Answer these questions.

- **What holiday did American Indians share with other Americans?**

- **Do all families celebrate the same holidays?**

- **How do people celebrate holidays?**

- **What are some holidays you know about?**

Work with your team.
Try one of these ideas.

➤ Make pictures of the holiday you chose. Show how families celebrate the holiday. Draw pictures of special foods they eat. Make models of the special things used to celebrate the holiday.

➤ Put your pictures in a book. Tell your classmates about the holiday. Show them your pictures. Tell them what people do.

Washington

Oregon

Idaho

Montana

North Dakota

South Dakota

Wyoming

Nebraska

west

Nevada

Utah

Colorado

Kans

California

Arizona

New Mexico

Oklah

Texas

Alaska

Hawaii

north

Maine

Vermont

New Hampshire

esota

Wisconsin

Michigan

New York

Massachusetts

Connecticut Rhode Island

Iowa

Pennsylvania

New Jersey

Illinois

Indiana

Ohio

Maryland

Delaware

Missouri

Washington, D.C.

West Virginia

Virginia

east

Kentucky

Tennessee

North Carolina

Arkansas

South Carolina

Mississippi

Alabama

Georgia

Louisiana

Florida

south

The United States

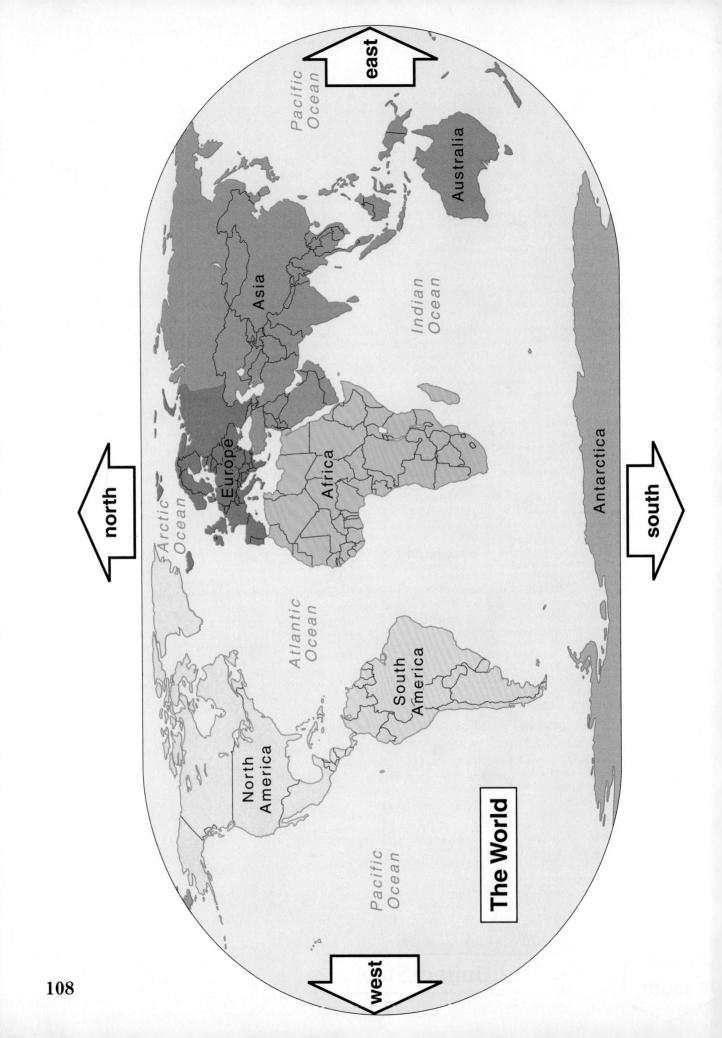

The World

Glossary

celebrate   (page 97)

chart   (page 94)

	First Thanksgiving	Thanksgiving Today
People	Pilgrims and American Indians	friends and family
Food	hunted for turkey	buy turkey in store
Time	three days	one day

directions   (page 61)

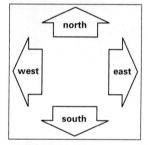

Earth   (page 69)

family   (page 6)

109

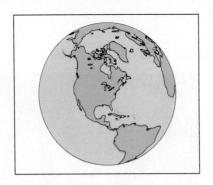 globe   (page 70)

 holidays   (page 97)

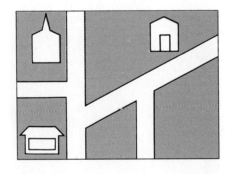 map   (page 60)

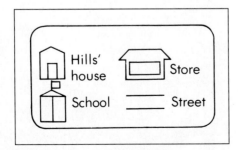 map key   (page 60)

mountains   (page 71)

need   (page 24)

neighborhood   (page 56)

picture graph   (page 52)

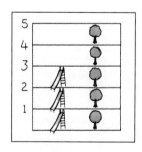

pollution   (page 80)

 resources   (page 77)

 rivers   (page 72)

 rules   (page 17)

 tepees   (page 89)

 want   (page 24)